FOIL HOLOCRINE

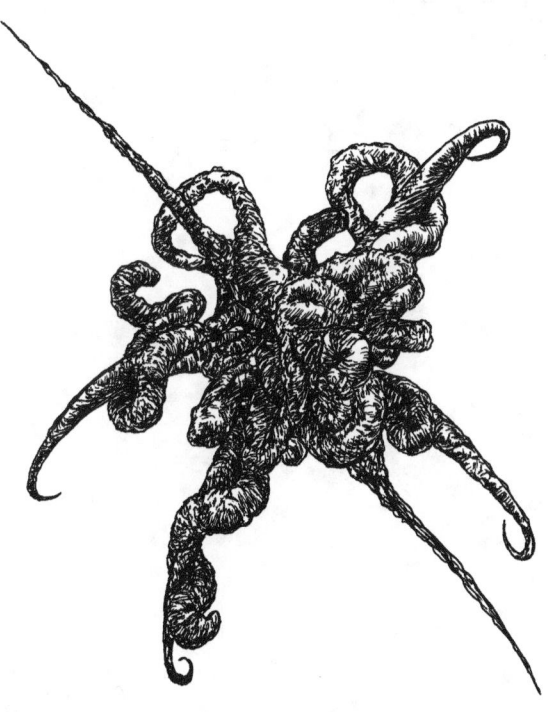

Foil Holocrine

Jenn Zahrt

REVELORE PRESS
SEATTLE
2019

FOIL HOLOCRINE

© Jenn Zahrt 2019.

All rights reserved. No part of this publication may be reproduced or utilized in any form or by any means, electronic or mechanical, including photocopying, recording, or by any information storage and retrieval system, without permission in writing from the Publishers.

Book design and cover illustration by Joseph Uccello

Interior illustrations: Thomas Brown II

ISBN: 978-1-947544-23-9

Printed in the United States of America

First printed by Revelore Press in 2019

Revelore Press
220 2nd Ave S #91
Seattle, WA 98104
United States

www.revelore.press

Nodules of literary shards contained;

Afterword, forward   7

Quarried:
- To break the habit of motorized living (lonely voltage)   10
- M-   11
- Circuits alive   12
- Entropic machine of perpetual motion   13
- Ulterior   15
- Hesitation   16
- Mute   18
- Immaculate Subservient Defiance   19
- Riot   21
- Cleavage   22
- Fore-pass   23

Imminent Remains:
- De-   25
- Caliber   27
- Patella   28
- Elliptic Mort   30
- Fuselage   31
- Cancer Misogyny   33
- Tempriority   35
- The Chase   37
- Discutted a citizen welt…   38
- Boomerang rupture   39

Ig-Knob-Leh	42
Polychromatic naked eye	43
Garnished tautology	45

Micro-prose:

Stagger, Quiver, Waggle, Nod	47
Ignore (fragment; *revised*)	47
There is a Hydrogen Bomb on your Raspberry Eyelid	48

Next level texts, 1999–2002:

Redivine	55
Oribatid	56
Merkliad	57

Micro-prose II:

I	60
II	61
III	61

Tiny Bullets:

[∗] **Alphambrosiomega**	64
[∗] Gentle infection	65

Afterword, forward:

I have become an intangible high-pitched noise. Five minutes spent in half-attention, but I remain unchanged. Keep looking for another dimension, interacting with the world around me and *waiting for the page to turn*. I was immediately injected into those pages last night. Fervor in the grandest sense of the word. Reactions cannot begin to explain this aftershock. An unsure look in the mirror to number that page? To assign a category to a scene in time… to stand for ten minutes, mouth agape, wishing to translate three-dimensional reality into one-dimensional words. I have crossed over this day into a new reality, my spirit transcends matter, as my story transcends linear writing, I have an inkling of proof in my soul. It is the last day of school before I to go Germany for a year. A threshold has been crossed and I have passed the test. And now I close my eyes and wait to imagine every page turning—the reality I sense is only a quarter of what is really there. Quite frankly, my filter has been torn, was torn, last night. I am ready for more. I can find more stimulation in what was once mundane. This anti-stasis of mentality. Transcending the present and therefore consuming the present in entirety.

<fin>
19.6.98

As *Foil Holocrine* finally makes its second print debut through Revelore Press, some words on its genesis are due. The original manuscript exuded spontaneously last millennium, in September 1997 in Vancouver, Washington, and has been processing, accreting for twenty years. In June of 1998, I broke into my parent's off-limits computer while they were out of town and typeset and printed the first edition using a single open MS Word document and never pressing save, leaving no digital trace. I wrote the paragraph on the previous page after this nearly twenty-hour publication excursion was complete and before I went to the print shop to create twelve copies. To my knowledge, only one extant copy remains. Material in the section titled 'Quarried' appeared in an experimental lit.pub called *The Quarry*, run by R. Mullard Jobson and his cohort of literary vandals. Their current whereabouts and remaining copies of *The Quarry* are unknown. Thanks to: the original Quarry horde for the impetus, Thomas Brown II for his illustrations, Joseph Uccello for his book design, and Wintermute Grey for everything. Finally, deep gratitude to the Emerald Quarry crew in Seattle, Washington for resurrecting the energy that enabled my first poems to precipitate.

Jenn Zahrt, PhD
Skyway, WA
18.7.18

QUARRIED

TO BREAK THE HABIT OF MOTORIZED LIVING (LONELY VOLTAGE)

ejecting electric spectrum
ego-matrix makes his studio, studious archway
                                    March day rising
Tantalizing rays reflect
rent.
                And the friends inspect
                The ends are bent
fast highway marching
                into water-land continuum
      his face a dime
space-time flow in him
                            rising force speed

remorse vacuum feeding
                receding at the c^2 value
voltage lonely hunter breeding
                        multiply sect repent
consume.
                Resume ejecting.

M -

dehydrated cornucopia of essentials
vessel of Armitage mussel
eyes wide to a Richter magnitude of eight
the landslide of body
buries the drought in abalone pus
Lymphatic hydration, infusion
Clams, when they boil,
crack open agoraphobic
bi-valves to escape,
and they magnify in the heat
much like the bloated starvation
of the Amazon swim.

CIRCUITS ALIVE

Circuits alive
within a 70 nanometer band width
implanting the future
the DNA sequence, altered, is.
Making labyrinth tunnels
deeper to the core.
hit
bicycle conception
the first creation
re-enacting

ENTROPIC MACHINE OF PERPETUAL MOTION

Run in place
    as if they were ejecting consuming and falling
                      around you
Infiltrate into the deepest abcess
    discover its maternal light
Absolute
    the imagination in concrete work and form
The sky absorbs your absence of color...
                    ...reflects your might
I can grasp you
    piece by piece inside me you go
Satisfy and deplete the incomplete protein cycle
    dissolving again you become whole
                In and out of it all.
Outside of you becomes in as I become out
    you compose me
Empathize until I see your metal wires,
               and bleed your tired heart
The source you were is a predator
    clamp onto the dear life you have left and
The possibilities are endless
In our state of total random static and equilibrium
                the annihilation survives
Quality is a one, where the void shall be a zero

    and I see with clarity how you respond

ULTERIOR

deadly thought infection
leaf blow your way through my skull
new dust and old words
into plasma
white cell life blood filling
stand tall
whispering a new revelation (#4)
clean minimalist fibers transmit
and not my mouth
but yours, speaks my thoughts

HESITATION

polish in the squalor
harbor resting making
festive nesting in between
the wave caressing
the possessive grave infesting
active action proton turning
with a burning fervent feeling
growing sky go forth abide
along a blow torch thigh inside
a scorching flyer in
the blaring sound completion
mound retrieval fairy ovum
life deletion in cohesion
holding restive festing evil

MUTE

    Siren
               wrapped in the arms of
                      Morpheus
Lay Midas Mercury leprechauns
    dip toes in Lethe
for she floweth forth
       Tiara
            and tendon before you.
Trojan labyrinths rise
        like   thick veins of phalli
    cover eyes   BLIND
        detonate smegma nuclear force
            so deep inside
Fast radiation spread in →
                the legs of Morpheus

IMMACULATE SUBSERVIENT DEFIANCE

Light ray
   defract slit
79° of freedom
spread waves under the floorboard
   tidal mortality
slips, the separated particles
massed together
   wet suction
Pierce the film
   membrane to the universe
I feel cold
I see light

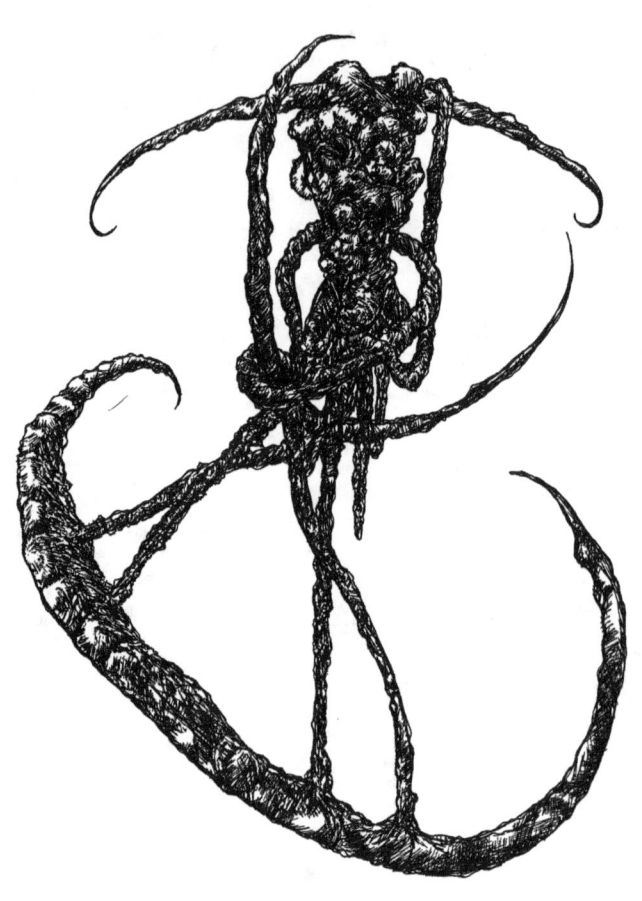

RIOT

an eye-glance,
approach to unknown
    she is opposing fresh conjuration and
    refusing to accept the invitation
arbitrary introduction of pleasure subsides
in the light she glows and transforms
    subcutaneous subterfuge
    evasion in the most subtle of formats
    pigments eject, turning membranes
    sour shades of curiosity and
    omnipotent repellents attack
    kamikaze in their silent motive
    undetected and too successful
    spawning rhino beetles of repulsion
arbitrary introduction of promise
fades to an ersatz glow of shallow water

CLEAVAGE

    existence,   peeling Fruit,
                      book sound,
                      SPLIT.
Shots fired cut, holes
   made   cleave
red brilliance enters the breast
        of street-side-walk-Fly
Wind continues in time
            to suck hair, leaves, trash, peels, Exit
                              stance
or the shiny days of (2 gauge steel)
        springs Fall.

FORE-PASS

A spring of evolution spinning out of
essential crevices
much denied occurrence
shaping miniature abstractions from all the
abundance
felt, tapping on a hidden light source.
documentaries
Aphids overpopulate the barren minefields of
activation catalysts, a smog trail rising,
perky noises past fences exhale.
A redundancy beyond circular motion.
Cement calls for the fertilization of
naked surface area.
A relic corroded by invisible dimensions.
Diabolical diameter. Neo-ill.
Intuitive magenta removal.
Contradiction efficiency upgraded by three,
the shot speed of stones skipping on milk,
this consensual vein of passage.
An alteration, contradiction, to THIS<
a row of mannequins succeeded in reeling in all
objects,
from both sides of the strip.

IMMINENT REMAINS

DE-

stigmatic mitochondrions
endostilettal suctionscale
offensified ostensity appropriated
by feudal stick figures
shifting in the fact of sneezing
genius. Laundry cornered and
trimmed by sinal conventions
dialogue (a heterogeneous mixture)
adhesive static uttering
stimulus process into the flesh
notably swamputrid at
sterilized capitations in
stoic thrombus,
Homunculoid monkrel.

FOIL HOLOCRINE

CALIBER

fusion
the difference of three and four
pressures stacking
connect<regrapple<gammatize,
niches unstiching fission
whipping exposed thin atom chains,
unit>rewrit>split and commit
attached: not to be admired
but to be destroyed in the eyes
only for the narcissistic reality
of graphite sheets through massacre
expiral altogether.
Room altitude a
jettison mystery relived on the LCD monitor.
Green hue played out in the wait
with lachrymal patients whining,
"lived near the ocean"
a sooty grab at skull entrance
slippery whettorn

NO lies on the couch
with certain tertian predilection
predictions of oncoming drill masochism
char and the taste of burnt tooth
left over after the chair.
presently the likeness imprinted
up there and before it.

PATELLA

widening to teragons of skates and rays
syllabolocious di-fuel compass
woven hemoglobin threads
relaxed
tarnished abandon of proportional function
icosahedral hip, trilobite
in length and extinction
opposing dine
absence lubricant
gem of bloodstone dabber
controlled peak inside elongation
logarithm preemptive
strandon testicle drip
gutteral eye nipple of corruption
erosion on the frontal motor vortex
latex forgets
nonchalant hymen cortex
skinny fingers relax and widen
searching excavations in wanton tunnels
blockage circumspect
resurrect.

ELLIPTIC MORT

Prickle puddle of encapsulating fantasy
dryly curbs the corner
whispy meniscus euthanasia!
the pump clot of the further trail
edged and denied errors.
force fed matter exercising entrance missions
with much descent and erupture
only assimilations accomplished
scar on the downflow rotary spittles four ejecticons:
an answering machine of the death call to be made
Expansion, A Crunchy Supernova!

FUSELAGE

conscious stream ebb and flowage counterfuge
backbreak the underfoot, the last rhyme sighing
whiskers mellow and consume
bare exposures with hyphae
an intertwining of cell bodies follows deeper
than geometric probabilities
surface vortex shaved with exacting pre-scission
slight enhancements, places carefully augmenting
the preferable behaviors, responses over come and
multiple delicacies awaiting discovery,
literal translation applicable…
torrid scenes raw, make the steel tremble
one form never expressed, and disposed of in every-
day glances,
the globe remaining a shock to the tired aftermath
of the cube worshipped.
curves, familiar tonalities in vocal transmissions,
wet keys, and unlocked secrets lie dormant
on the doormat, waiting for ring worm attack into
frequent erogenous glances of imaginary tapestries
pathways open to insidious capture
initiate the in-layer, or lay in the initiation,
weakness in the grapple: quiver:lips:sight:mental
exaggeration to the point of tangible sustenance
physical hunger for the taste, muscular deprivation
but a side effect to the opinion

the limits attract form,
full circular expanse of tense skin
breeze scapegoated for the understated reality
entirely possible to walk and know this out of sheer
lack of mass? shape including physical entrances?
critical disagreements, contrast
looming on the horizon of the back, walks a fly, spy
to the pheremone made
when goal and imagery bleed together,
a tilted wet masterpiece.

CANCER MISOGYNY

Philoprogenetive energy leaks into the
 micrometer
exuding out of vessels,
ships to an era of ignorance,
SHE IS THE HARBINGER
muddy watts and stained similies
dropped casually out the door,
portal to the present.
consensually available echoes
threaten the unwanted actuality
an experience intimidated by the moon's
 reflection in
the word Mother,
M for murder,
the shape of lip pursed in superiority
assimilated into the opposed idea
feeding the drive
continued stares into the
INCOMPREHENSIBLE realness
faded lights reflect the intensity of attention span,
no one else can know,
sharp lands built upon the dead bodies of
 plankton,
green food to the baby nests
soggy, the intention of goodwill
gnashing tendency held back by an understanding

of MORAL CONDUCT?

a curiosity of smells enticing, wanting to lick the
vapir of this WOMAN's sweat?

what neurology possesses itself in her legs?

fingertips of clue spring in quotes, subtitles,

everpresent phenom,

manifested in yet another body,

reflections of the crab,

crib

wholly evil haunting,

the continuous escape and entrance of

maternal crustaceans.

TEMPRIORITY

An inanimate whiteness
so undeniably aware of itself that
it takes showers in its prudence.
Daily
Defying
Hatchet breath rewind
vagabond ecliptic mobster
lunking, a machete withdrawn
cop and you late
kinetic transfusion of transcendental
overhead
green glow worms writhe in piles
Naked breast exposed for parental
    guidance chat
one more step, plunge
another imitation,
lilac meat heaps
fumage sheet, reaping sex odors out of
unwilling pores
cores of whiteness exhuming
an unbearable string of metallic thoughts
coagulated into galaxies of conversational
topography
an iron red blood essay,
a machete withdrawn
prudent showers

in
animate
whiteness.

THE CHASE

Oval undulation
moist humor; secretion
of the excited kind.
Building stretchable monuments
animation waiting to be played out
anticipation in the biology of the
vaginal organ.

DISCUTTED A CITIZEN WELT...

Concave bereaved
delivered in a circular package
understood in a slight wrist flick
slumage peacock
hoarding room herd together
it was street light
destructive radiation relys on skin
thus far: two feet remained placid
elastic to the dirtless concretion
a featherotic
work stops along passageways leading
lead and anthologous to the rule
thumbing pages scattered increase in population
as it writ: circular in packagery
De-livered. A cancer patient
expulsion out of womb's entrance
yes:
belly buttons evolute into erogenous timezones
concaved
tuft of follicle rumpled: air suck
eye slide left.   Right he was
and grey-blue stood the color upon him
signature was missing a letter
neon sign with all R's missing.

BOOMERANG RUPTURE

Defects in the matrix
spermatic harpsichord
Dischordian and scored
scalpel peeling two sides open
all fistulous tumours falling
in those members only
complaints caused by wet feet
moving viral cocci and spherical
in globular atlas tribute
creasing lines envelop like longitude
restricted advance inasmuch as
the harm done can be mirrored back
the scar closes and data flows

IG-KNOB-LEH

Cornea dice birthed
colarboration galactica
an absence of viral tolerance
cholera chamomile chiffon
a surrender diagonal
cryptic acryllation
constellations of destitute imaginings
fleshed out twice dimensional to
a defunct tri-perception
subcortextural prefunctory instincts
achieved only through practice
learned and traded among charlatans
discombobulous flavors entice the others
festive occasions oceanic gathering clumps
anvil weakens with recital
unison of wavelengths cut to no crate
smell foreskin, bulbous light fixture
scape bloated extremity

POLYCHROMATIC NAKED EYE

Symmetrical meter shortened by the sequel
sixty oranges roast in new ways
thought of, but never implemented
skint and scented
carbonous resins release strength
the foil, aluminum conductor of trains,
underground in tunnels those trains,
those fontescapes,
a whisper in the tubes, hairs line a crowd,
wave secrets deciphered, the organ of all organs,
not to be stretched out, but taken for granted.
message is clear, despite spiteful effort,
one negative charge responds,
and a positive flow circumplates,
mutual reception of a concept,
complexities
inverse to the temperature of any system.
Tetraspheres of carbon line every tissue,
and carbonated beverage lines intestines.
depleting the nature of the actual purpose
using the degree as an excuse to copulate
habits, habits
unites move in telepathic unison,
only when the orders are of a
homosympathetic language,

any other and an orbital of sixty corners in
    produced
strength beyond centuries
harlot seed,
comprehension carved out of
halves of a navel-less species.

GARNISHED TAUTOLOGY

Tepid sepia stretch-marks. Misanthropinion,
a shallow waltz of lightening.
Encompass the close view.
A weapon designed for
agrarian agoraphobes.
Silent.
Move the bile of anxiety to South Dakota.
It was a decoy anyway.
Hail
those intrepid Vikings! Lechery to stark.
Open yonder.
Young, fallow malts keep brightening.
Pompous.
The chode through a stamen of that broken
mirror.
Utilitarian demeanor. cleaner.
The pubis of a young calf stretching
uncircumcision
into female mouths of indecision.
Let the batteries bombard.
The lukewarm fingerprint, bitten at the core.

MICRO-PROSE

STAGGER, QUIVER, WAGGLE, NOD

An incoherence as precise as the tether of protein markedly extending twither from the curd and whey of her increasing blouse. A loose disdain for things material but nonetheless necessary. It was brought to her attention with a wordless gesture of clarification. The finger extension, a hyperexcited glance of intrusion, prodded her wide middle region, a thorax of illustrious luggage waterfalling into abdominal fullness. Her right hand was yet extended, a flat surface. She held fresh meat on a tray in an Egyptian pose, right angles exceeding morality and acceptance. The cocky angular chin restricting downward motion. What is this catenation, a viral invasion of proper ascension and truthful declanation? Groping for a recollection. A smack grip catch! Crab mouth men!

IGNORE
(fragment; *revised*)

The cells divide like a crowd being bombed, an air raid running smooth through a mass of people. Tiny capillaries between these cells break by the thousands. Eventually the blade hits a solid vein. The cell-body is full of adrenaline, the heart pumps wide and fast, fear. Crimson rushes out of the broken irrigation system, geyserlike. It continues spreading in the wake of the razor's edge.

Cold, sharp steel glides deeper into the fleshy mass. Bone not expecting to wedge a ragged piece of metal 45 degrees into its brittle structure. Pain shoots up into the center nerve center of his brain. Deep below, a rugged knife splits his thigh in two. On his face lies the closest thing to awe, more than agony. His eyes look down, dilated, and on the corner of his mouth, a grin peeks through. The porcelain around him pools with flowing blood. His body smacks to the hard surface.

Bloodloss prevents rational thought. He opens up his blue lips and lets a rush of cells, encased, red, plasma, fill his mouth. In a last gasp, he swallows, lathered in a warm crimson bath. The tub is full now. His head, heavy and submerged, empty shell, chrome blade.

Another thin hand reaches in, ripping at the drain plug, opaque red making it hard to find.

THERE IS A HYDROGEN BOMB ON YOUR RASPBERRY EYELID

Linear entrances are escaped to make room for spiraled crossovers and run-throughs. A bonding specific to the shape of enzymes. Undeserving. They had the ability to see the reflections, and ignored the power of the sense. A number beyond calculation was hated unconsciously, and it lay itself open only to her.

On rooftops and deserted roadways, she would, in times of chemical storms, spread her legs across the sky to take in the pieces. If those ways could be set in her every cell, an achievement above superstitious palm tree shade could be wrought. No longer chains constructing a cycle of indigestion. She wants to see the sun in the most abstract way possible, farthest from firsthand the better. And she was on her way…

A lapping tongue wrinkling around submissive liquid. Yellow flicker of petal drop, chord strung and muscle prompt upward. The final lick.

Suggesting movement, the assembly diagonally divides to escape eye contact. But the watch still reads 12:42. On the horizon, after the vaginal crevice that has been carved out of centuries of river existence, a UV ray is recognized as day. The claustrophobic nature of the government stood. Walls to be built up again.

More roof. An official decree to change the color of the atmosphere! The obvious lyrics ring too often. Shouting unison vocabulary to the proper figurehead, again, the burnt edges are passed by. Bullet proof glass serving its purpose. The watch/12:42. Desensitized to guns among acute sensing of knives!

Expansion and contraction; the breath of the lung the universe is! But wasn't he right when he said it would contract!

And it is. One day she will have captured the sun from infinite positions, reflected in tin cans on the beach, the muted shine of brick walls.

Assembly harasses the conquistador and his push pin mistress. A compunctual reliance on the sex of animals. He was really a photographer.

A concession made because her lip sallowed so carefully. The crease part opened in a calculated simulation of arched feathers. He liked the skin texture of the chin. At least she was a rotten flamingo, barely aborbing the color of the food she ate, in her renegade consumption. She was reading.

Her skin displayed poor nutrition. A beak protruding from his aura longed to apprentice her, teach nutritional habits, to coddle her and feed her chewed morsels. Line after letter and word, the pauses of the space bar, she kept reading. Or was it the headphones. He took his shoes off. The spark on the winged insect's mechanism defracted an energy ray and ricocheted the wave off of a window angled toward the vehicle. The E lit up and devoured the word, she went blind for a second as the bus broke off the matrimony of light and page, her eyes proceeded along with the speed limit of the road. He would have bought her some carrots.

An abrupt stop brought her electronics to a halt and a yellow tape tug to accompany her exit. Limp hair echoed to him, follow her. Vacant sentience entering physical residence…THEN…She stood on a platform in the middle of the room and spat out a sentence that shot through the heads and executed war with collective morality, a collection begun from the first exposure to that white light and true inhalation. A cough full with mucus of womb and fetus. This statement so profound and simplicit. It spun tops and cartwheels of ideological carnage out of all systems, a discreet spin cycle of turntable echo:

"Direction is emoted from the whiplash corner of a remote lack of control"...

...and she broke a thin, young tube of glass, releasing a chasm of sperm into the heavy air. All around her watched as the descending pictures came from the ceiling, lathered in blue ejectiles holding each snapshot.

"Bidding starts at 20,000"

Everyone reached for their respective walls. Enclosing the glittered audience in solitaire sardine caskets, his view of her was obstructed and all that was left, her bare foot in the air. She imploded; her voice an integral fuse inside his finger. Shaking entrance into the wallpaper of auctionary fixtures. He noticed a special flick of memory as the picture tore between his arms. Submissive riot, they all relished in the approval. Shard of pulp, and they were one on the platform; frozen encapsulation of 20,000. Reduced to 11,010 after implosion. Assimilation. I closed my eyes and stepped out of my pencil sharpener. The phone cord was my communicatory intestine. I am a song of hybrid motion. Mannerisms of lactation draw in rejected catheters. The tardy progression of the seed production was halted because of her absorption. Lucid terminals continue evacuation into her spongy womb. A broken water. Small pod vomited, bulemic onto sheets of prime metal...Proper...The flick at the end of her flooded hair, descending cascade of droplets. A landscape, steel vegetable lush caught the inescapable blue tendencies of the desolate wind. Her violent heartbeat timing the drip from her amphibious locks. A percentage of her iridescent scales fall down, and she moves on, all fours. The puddle of her emergent body was left five feet behind her as her lilac face…

…and she drooled, thought to herself "I will sleep with the urgency of urination between my legs." Hairs struck her back and stomach. She was shredding by the ashram. A furnace slug of shoes turned the opposite way of how one takes them off when they enter a Japanese bordello. She was staring at burning sticks through a lens of dog slobber. It was the deliberate mass of glowing sarcasm. They suffocated in the atmosphere of her dilated pupil…

…silence allows room for:

She stood, a diamond on her shoulder, dressing her in vinegar. She stood long enough to transport her brainwave into his hands. Willpower overtook; a semi-expected answer. A special penetration into a different tongue would have been the outcome; their embrace reflected on the chandelier, and increased into the vortex, the continuous equal of other dimensions. No such entrance was made. Proper spoken word occurred and a shoulder tap separated forward movement…

…the glare penetrates her eyelids. She looks over the rooftop to the asphalt below. The tops of all the cars stare at her with bleached white rays of sunlight. Tiny reflections of the star make themselves known, they do not discriminate and allow phosphorescent halos from the deepest black void. It burns deep into the skull, claiming her, singeing her hair.

She is the X quotient, the variable, the volatile chemical. Her claws have groped and scaled…

…Her silk gown billows; harsh light blinds, empty hands.

<fin>

NEXT LEVEL TEXTS
1999–2002

REDIVINE

Frust ratio: number eclipse
-ling fluke delve oblanceolate pelvis
corp arbitrate blotches ankle crack
smouldering ink castles on vice cakes
mode: only ice skates relate to road.
blendance of retread cusp margins
lisps retraced to endings to prove
heavy acid bow ties choke idiolect:
must disambiguate the virid immediacy
null, null rhombus transportation to show
glow past dawn lawn fry.
grid baseboard antler harness.
Focus. Stand still.

ORIBATID

Athalon tripod parliamentary
rapid obstacle appearance
rudimentary die squad decathlon
irrigation deity predistilled
chamber switch highlight enrapture
sights secured,
        a peltry pentad awaiting
make the kill
        manipular destrier
        landfill, landfill

MERKLIAD

rage on the curled lip, feeling wind resistance

gull

ornery ort peddle dropped useless now
unapproachable meat barker.
inscisor intuition, best to let bacteriophage be.
empty vescular gut moves on.

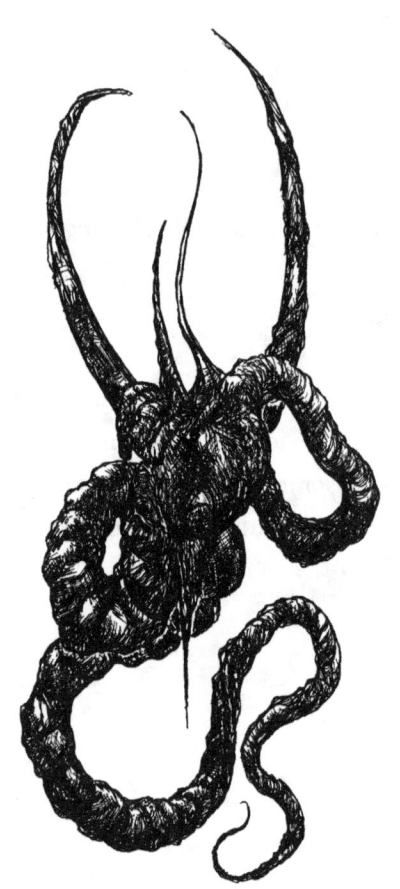

MICRO-PROSE II

I

Blotches, seamless and seemingly harmful to the health of an evicted state of mind. But the evasion of the cosine depths would last no more and a new replacement for the legs of broken stools would have to suffice the Assembly and the expectancy of a semblance of elevator-politic-emancipation…

…The building fracture bled along dry muscles. Escalation derived from exclamatory measures. The ceiling notes the comprehension of a windowless existence, alas the corporeal desire is not of a railway-bloated cremation. Lick, a purple scone to mask all swimming possibilities. British generals specify to which country their due letters will be sent, a courier travels in a heat of blackness to be killed upon arrival, but the crystal envelopes ring true and the wanton life is rewarded with another at the paleontologist so secretly hidden in the mealtimes of forgotten culture lying static on the Madegascar coast. It was the collected spewings of migrant autonomy that compromised the ribbon strings of the woman who only too gladly participated in the twelve-night excuse for a fortnight celebration. An event casted to recall the return rate of the year's past smoke signals to a deaf man, a life loathsome on a barren hillside devoted to ephemeral documentation of gaseous marbles. It was not that the method wasn't correct, it just so happened that another's will became so clearly defined that all else ceased to exist, and a new expansion out of this conceptual masking forced a contraction

that devoured all meaningless treasures. A ground
zero hero triumphant created dissidence and a set
of black hole earrings for his bridal excursions. No
longer Japanese brine came from the tap faucet;
her was a performance of a beaded vocal war, triggering standing ovulations across the new peripheral audience…

II

Perils, these Afghanistan wings chewing the
cud of a stream made of pearls. This wade changes
the tides that will wash the faces of our soft ladels.
Corroded on the barrier, too tall, deteriorated in
the hand lotion smoothness of their thoughts. This
whithered weapon will explode all exteriors, rip
the dilated necklaces off the conquistador and his
bloated laws. Not said, but done.

III

A powder rising in the pump. A clog to amass all
seasons. How does the chemical produce the lion,
the intrigue, the valor. A step goes by and the right
hand moves a fraction. An imminent repetition of
the moment over a certain space. The legs of the
world were intertwined, wrapped around toilets,
lovers, and nooses. A memory, relative, peeks into
the stronger magnitudes residing as a membrane
in all humans. The fractals have a sense, properties,
real estate in time, they own and barter. Motion is
the played out hypothetical transfers of these plots

of income. As many fractals as can be imagined, twice that many exist. A human hand is the hologram for existence, yet so is an oil spill. Perspective must be retained. Pixels evolve, they always stay pixels, but colors in them pass through all transparencies. So does fortitude pass through.

TINY BULLETS

- The eternal light of mastication, the orts of what could have been mammoth entities.

ALPHAMBROSIOMEGA

- Systems cyst
  mungous hue spread
  re-read spree in spring
  inspiring, tiring tristans
  lung, us through thems'
  decree less wiring
  junkless hum, let go
  retiring

- Deviant in color: The snow turned a violet shade of purity in combat. It is not seen on things that end. It is not noticed by the regulars.

GENTLE INFECTION

- Aphid infection forming
  filmy predilection
  swarming
  affecting the quiet regime
  brudely spayedless.

- The room was a compound of the synastry of four. The only rampage allowed was the hideous clasping of tea in the throat. Mouths Open…

  <fin>

FOIL HOLOCRINE WAS TYPESET IN NEW VELJOVIC, DESIGNED BY JOVICA VELJOVIĆ.

www.ingramcontent.com/pod-product-compliance
Lightning Source LLC
Chambersburg PA
CBHW052104110526
44591CB00013B/2349

PRAISE FOR
hell of birds

"*hell of birds* is ferocious in its energy and acrobatics. With arresting images and unexpected enjambment, the poems twist and turn, often coming to a halt so surprising, you're left reeling in the white space, out of breath. Kimberly writes, 'One day the world will sing through your blood.' After reading this collection, you'll feel the earth in your bones."

— Erica Dawson,
author of *When Rap Spoke Straight to God*

"You've not read a collection like *hell of birds* before. This is wild new work by a poet with a vision and a voice—and with wings. The rapture is contagious: it's our lives. These poems net all of it—the heaven and the hell of it in these fearless and music-filled poems."

— Laura Kasischke,
National Book Critics Circle Award winner

HELL OF BIRDS
KIMBERLY POVLOSKI

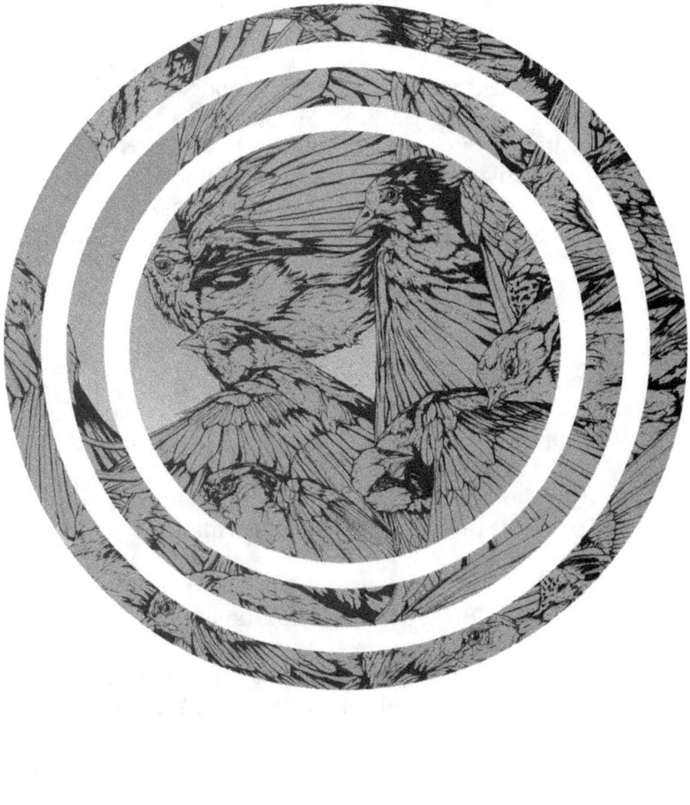

Independently published by *Driftwood Press*
in the United States of America.

Managing Poetry Editor: Jerrod Schwarz
Poetry Editor: Megan Krupa
Interior Design & Copyeditor: James McNulty
Cover Image: Alexander Landerman
Cover Design: Sally Franckowiak
Fonts: Existence, Merriweather, Garamond, & Cinzel.

Copyright © 2019 by Kimberly Povloski
All Rights Reserved.

No part of this publication
may be reproduced, stored in a retrieval
program, or transmitted, in any form or by
any means (electronic, mechanical,
photographic, recording, etc.), without
the publisher's written permission.

First published in March 2019
ISBN-13: 978-1-949-06502-2

Please visit our website at www.driftwoodpress.com
or email us at editor@driftwoodpress.net.

contents

i. 1
    transfiguration 3
    dogwood dream 5
    pensive no. 1 7
    cotton nero a.x 8
    pensive no. 2 9
    pearl 10
    nighthawk 11
    home poem 12

ii. bird gods 15
    the ontology 17
    indigo bunting 17
        chorus, sung by birds 17
    ornithomancy 18
    field dressing 19
    painted bunting 19
    funeral for the great horned bird 20
    a chronology from *St. Cuthbert of the Crows* 21
        chorus, sung by birds 22
    ornithomancy 22
    history of dark jay 23
    a hagiography 24

interview 27

i .

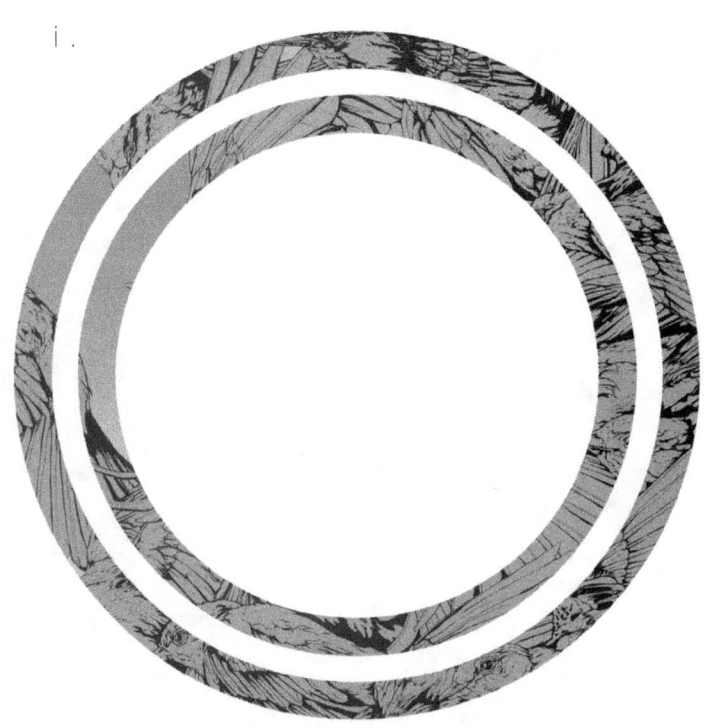

transfiguration

the dazzling
monstrosity
of eyes
of moth's
wings

      danced across
      the ceiling

and like
Moses-
on-the-mountain
we dared not move
when the hand of night
came down
to close
our eyes

      we spent forty days
      dreaming in the dust

when we woke
we felt no pain

      only strangeness
      in the twilight

and we could not
understand then

      the transfiguration
      that had taken place

why we had to turn away
from our own image
in the glass

      or the perversion
      of the shadow
      that cast itself
      across the bed
      where we once
      slept

        but now
        only lie
        in darkness
        listening to
        sounds

sometimes
our own voice
whispering
prayer

        sometimes
        the shadow
        mimicking
        speech
        back at us

always
the soft
hysterical
bodies
of moths
beating
themselves
against
the glass

        the scales
        of their wings
        shattered

            like Moses'
            stone tablets

        words of God
        that slipped
        away
        and
        left us
        alone

to fear

dogwood dream

i.

light upon
the oil black oil
bird wings
broke
into as many
colors as there are
faces of angel
who spoke
perturbations
through the gates
of ivory
and horn

ii.

harbinger flew into the face of the sun and laughed

he found the singularity

>   the secret place
>   of wound-
>   that-will-not-heal
>   by probing
>   with his fingers
>   deep
>   into
>   your
>   personal
>   body

>   which afterwards
>   you realized

you no longer wanted to keep

iii.

something bright
as the taste
of blood
cloistered around   your head
                        your neck
                        your thighs
                        and left
                        your breasts
                        bare

much like a halo

           which the thrush
               cannot penetrate

though he has watched you for years
from the branches of a dogwood tree

               that is burning now
                   with his wings

iv.

several of his faces
saw you in the morning
    and grinned

                   one looked away

pensive no. 1

back into the
shallows of it—
     smells of salt
        and pine.
lungs white
as the ditch-lilies
that blurr by the
side of the road
leading here.

     the forest
    hollowed out
     with
hulked tropic
lightning,
     diaphanous
      thunder.

who stood here.
who burned it
down. who are
we burying
today. who
struck & what
shattered. child.
who dwells amid
their terrors. who
taught you to
smoke?

[no-way] is
home.
    dark pearl of
     weather.

the wisdom of it
bristles under
your tongue.

cotton nero a.x

i.   cleanness

hum of summer sleep blurs itself in
the gemmish facets of your organs

you bed down on burrs
and dream of your sister
planting teeth
beside a river you can't
cross to save her

ii.   patience

for now you just want to hunt blackbirds
with a long sharp stick that whistles
when it wings through air

you want to tip their breasts with blood

iii.   pearl

come stalking in on sly feet
fawnsoft and smooth as afterbirth

pensive no. 2

One day
you
will be stung
awake by the
most beautiful
bees, Old
World and
orange as the
harvest moon
hung in its
own violent
ripple of color.

One day the
world will sing
through your
blood.

p e a r l

The summer your parents planted a wisteria tree it died.
Remember your mother's grief, her body
in bed and no lights—a wounded shape.   Crouching
in the banana leaves and calla lilies, you caught spiders
in empty Gerber baby jars, too young to understand
what you knew. On the night the French bread somehow
caught fire, dinner was ruined when your mother said *My
life is like this bread.*   Your father left it outside
to smolder in the rain.

The soupy spaghetti you stared into.

Days later, in bedroom dark, she was quiet again and you
didn't want to startle her. You asked *Mama, is your dome
cracked*—a line from a show you both knew—and she
laughed.

n i g h t h a w k

mothish small
&suffers the coyote's suffering
      the dustbite and bedraggle
prairie mange
winged fang
      stumble on down
into the ditch
dead ditch dog
      we name a town Nighthawk
          just to abandon it
we name a place and
      its mimetic
mask of ash
white ash
the sun-scalded ashes to ash
      its monstrosity of eyes
weeping
among trees
      so lonely
in its crypsis
      we name a thing
watch it
h o/a llow it-
      self
out

home poem

guest saint a broken window

pieces of bright caught
in the garden's leafy throat

a yellow extinction

a mercy to pearl away
in stomach acids, alkaloids

a mercy   growing
among eggshells and chicken bone

        aconite
the green shaft glissant

dreamspear, devil's helmet
moonmaw, monkshood

i kept it
        a relic

and the doors rusted down
and the mirror in the hall
and the hall clotted with dust
and the glass an utterance
and the garden swallowing it
and the light on all fours

like an animal
i carry it always with me
        on my back

ii. bird gods

the ontology

as from the dark burst heart of earth
a mudswallow disgorged itself from the shadow
under a bridge
        and flew through me   until

i was pinned open

on needles
with the eyes bright
and my insides   a cloud of dust
across the dry spangled grass
soft as lying down   as mouthing yellow flame

indigo bunting

above me the sky was quaking`

chorus, sung by birds

there is no shadow of turning with Thee

ornithomancy

a young owl eating moths
his eyes bright in the heady moons of headlights

i see him swallow sisters—

>*Ascalapha odorata*
>*Thysania aggripina*

i will later find their bodies
crushed in the backseat of my car
at the bottom of my laundry basket, folded into
velvet stuck to the mirror at the foot of my bed

field dressing

(there are
frightful landscapes
painted in
her eyes)

painted bunting

i could set fire
to these fields

i could burn

funeral for the great horned bird

storm clouds will gather
spin glass glowered
and reach with pale blade of light
to cut fire into his wings

a chronology from
St. Cuthbert of the Crows

I. How he foresaw a vision of Fire coming from the Devil
II. How he sowed a field with wheat and could not keep the birds from it
III. How, when the field was really set on fire, he could not put out the fire
IV. How the Crows did not apologize for the injury they had done

chorus, sung by birds

there is no shadow of turning with Thee

ornithomancy

struck down

>he hid his face from the sky

>he pressed his eyes into the dirt
>and searched for
>a mother

>he was suffering in the heat

>he had a mighty need
>to return

there was smoke

history of dark jay

it is a hatred from the heart of the sky
      hulked on all fours
           over gaea

wearing the sleek corvid grin
      that cleaves space between her eyes
           and chin

in which he sets a fire

his shadow is a burn

a hagiography

WHEN I found her discharged in the red
clay, she closed her eyes   and lullaby
was hush of blackbirds among firs. Here also,
as elsewhere, I would go forth, when others
were asleep, to spend the night in watchfulness
and return home at the hour of matins, dawn-solemn
and without words. For I had loved the Lord,
and with much sorrow saw the hawk-headed one flee
from the fields at first flame, leaving only a dark char,
an idol of himself, to mock me,   orgasmically,   over
and over   again.   Therefore, I asked the earth:

Who now will commend these burnt bones to the sea?
Ought I not eat ash.

AGAINST THE IMPOSITION OF SILENCE
a conversation with
Kimberly Povloski & Jerrod Schwarz

I wanted to start our conversation of hell of birds with, you guessed it, birds. The poems in this collection do not shy away from the quiet, mystic, and sometimes grotesque world of fowl. What is your personal connection to birds?

I wouldn't say that I have a *personal* connection. I feel like an observer, or even a witness, of birds and bird behavior. They're as wild as wolves, yet so familiar. They exist and thrive in human-engineered environments—in the cities and suburbs that have destroyed their natural habitats. That adaptability, that cunning, seems almost elemental. Birds-as-animal embody an extant wilderness in our daily lives. I think that's what makes birds-as-symbol so provocative.

As a reader, I felt the same way. I was a witness to destruction, always slightly adjacent to the grotesque. How do you see the poems' speaker interacting within the world you've created?

So I have to admit that, in general, I have a more active awareness of voice than I do the role of the speaker in my own work. I think of the speaker as subconscious interloper, a kind of interference that occurs during writing. The speaker shifts the poem depending on the angles of observation and illumination, like what happens in the moment of iridescence. I guess that's an attempt to answer the question from a "craft perspective," as a poet.

Looking at these poems as a reader, the speaker seems sibylline. Like the Pythia, or one of the mystics of the Middle Ages (Hildegard von Bingen, Julian of Norwich, Teresa of Avila), the speaker experiences the world beyond an "objective" reality. She exists, synchronistically, in the realm of perceivable sense-data and in the realm of apocalyptic vision. And like those other women, it's her role to bear the suffering of witness and then interpret that suffering for the reader.

This concept of interpreting suffering is maybe most evident and striking in "a chronology from *St. Cuthbert of the Crows*." When you started writing *hell of birds*, did you intend to place any mystic figures directly within the po-

ems? Does this collection share any of the goals of those medieval mystic's writings?

Did I intend to place any mystic figures directly into the poems? Not really. I would say that it was more incidental than intentional.

For me, the creative process begins with reading and research. Then there's the work of analysis and synthesis before ever writing anything down. Synthesis is the most intense part of the process. It's where the language of the poem works itself out. I can bring my own experiences to the poem. I can bring an understanding of those experiences. But they can't be the only factors—otherwise, I'd be writing nonfiction. During synthesis, the subconscious is forging connections between inner and outer knowledge, puzzling out the signified, identifying the signs, and creating the symbols that become the language of the poem.

"bird gods," the long poem that contains "a chronology...", was originally a much shorter poem about driving through Texas prairieland in autumn to visit an abusive boyfriend. I worked with it for months—and by that, I mean I read voraciously and rewrote the same ten lines over and over until the rest of the poem yielded itself to language. Finishing "bird gods" is what made me realize that hell of birds was waiting to happen.

What I started with and what the poem ended up being are two completely different things. I was reading *Scivias, Philokalia,* and some really weird, still sort of pagan, Celtic hagiography around that time. Passages from *The Book of the Dead. Purgatorio* (the Ciardi translation). Sean Bishop's collection, *The Night We're Not Sleeping In.* There were lots of articles about dark matter and quantum physics, too. Stuff about bugs. What I read provided me with a different way of understanding my experiences and helped to move my poems from the idiosyncratic to something, hopefully, more universal.

That movement towards the universal, towards the "Other," is something that I believe my collection shares with the writings of the medieval mystics. We confront pain, suffering, and trauma; we confront the ideas of chaos and absence in a world that is spiritually rife. We are violated. Our sense of self is overrun. It's shattered. We are looking for someone to be held accountable. The mystics find their solace in the Other. "All shall be well, and all shall be well, and all manner of thing shall be well." They are remade. They become saints. They are themselves and more than themselves. My poems don't reflect that same peace, or completeness. My speaker survives as an extant, grappling with a question of regression: what if this has made me into an animal? A Callisto instead of a Catherine.

Very similar to Aase Berg's poetry, there is a tender horror to the personification of animals in your writing, such as moths with "soft / hysterical / bodies" and an owl that can "swallow sisters." How do these moments of human embodiment fit into the overall narrative of *hell of birds*?

Oh, wow. We studied Berg's *With Deer* in my first poetry workshop. It was one of the first books of contemporary poetry I ever read. So can I just say how delighted I am at that comparison? Thank you.

I think that those moments are probing the distinction between "animal" and "human" nature. It's an interrogation of those terms. It's a reaction to the monstrosity that humanity can harbor.

You could also explain it as a kind of Romanticism. Maybe the moths are embodying the speaker's emotion. Maybe the speaker has been brought to the point that she can witness the moths in their own terror, and that connects them. I couldn't say for certain.

Beyond the wonderful imagery and subject matter of the collection, I really appreciated your attention to line length. Specifically, I love how the majority of poems make use of deftly short lines, but the last poem "a hagiography" sprawls in comparison. Given the title (hagiographies are biographies of saints) and its explicit summon of spiritual lives, what is the significance of this final visual change?

I was attempting to mimic the style and tone of real hagiographies. I wanted the sense of gravitas you often intuit from antique Latin, its array of sadness and solemnity and taxonomical precision. I felt like it would balance the language of the poem and help to bring a sense of finality to all of the voices and perspectives at work in "bird gods."

How long had you been working on this collection? What poems, structures, or ideas didn't make it into the final manuscript, and why were they cut?

I wrote most of *hell of birds* during the second-to-last quarter of my thesis year and worked on editing the poems in my final quarter. So that's about three months of writing and three months of editing. Probably less. It happened so quickly. I really, honestly, needed poems for my thesis, so that certainly moved me along. Once I got started, the writing became very organic. And it was exciting. I felt like I knew what I was doing, which is kind of a rare feeling for a graduate student.

"transfiguration" and "dogwood dream" are the only poems in *hell of birds* that weren't explicitly written for the manuscript. They're among the first real poems I ever wrote, so that dates them to 2014? 2015?

As I said earlier, "bird gods" was the catalyst for writing this collection. After finishing that poem, I knew that *hell of birds* was waiting to happen. I also knew that I wanted "bird gods" to be in its own section. I *really* wanted it to be the first poem of the collection. When you study ancient cultures, you often begin by looking at their mythological texts. The stories that people tell about themselves and their origins can often give us more insight into their lives than what ends up getting recorded as "history." It's the difference between "who we are" and "what we did and what was done to us." Or, maybe, "who we think we are" and "what we want you to know about what we did and what was done to us." So you read Homer before Herodotus. You rely on the mythology to foreshadow and explain the history. I see "bird gods" as the mythological counterpart to the personal accounts/childhood poems collected in the other half of the manuscript. The original order was switched because, as my friend and fellow poet, Taylor D. Waring, pointed out, "bird gods" isn't the most accessible of poems. It needs some introduction. I think that was really good advice.

For the most part, *hell of birds* was a fully realized project. I didn't have a lot of excess material. I thought about writing a whole series of surrealist *visio* poems based on medieval manuscripts like *Cotton Nero A.x*, but I think that's the only idea that wasn't followed to fruition.

Where does *hell of birds* stand in the scope of your writing? Is this collection indicative of your poetry as a whole or do those poems hold a unique place in your personal catalogue?

It's kind of hard to reflect on the scope of my writing. I haven't been doing this for very long and I still have a lot to learn. If this collection is indicative of anything, I hope that it's how I try to approach poetry and even language itself. Thomas Merton said that the original primary function of language was to bear witness to the hidden meaning of a thing, rather than to "talk about" or around it. Language that bears witness is poetry. I call myself a poet because I want to struggle every day with my ability to look at a thing and, with patience and compassion, see to the soul of it.

These poems never shy away from the brutal questions of spirituality and suffering. What advice would you give to any writers who might be writing from a similar place?

I don't think I'm really in a position to give anyone advice, but I do believe that it was really important for me to learn to stop "shying away" from things—artistically and intellectually.

I grew up being told that I was too sensitive, too serious, too dramatic. Whenever I was upset, I was told that I needed to grow a thicker skin. If I was vulnerable, it was my own fault. Once, a man in a grocery store put his hand down his pants as he approached me and started asking me questions about myself. "How old are you? Do you need help finding anything? I can show you what you want." I was thirteen. I ran. When I found the people who I thought would protect me, they told me I was overreacting. So I learned to shut up. I stopped confiding in people when I felt hurt, afraid, or threatened—by men, especially. I learned that my pain made me detestable, that I was unbelievable, so I said nothing.

When I started writing poetry, I was rebelling against the imposition of silence trained on me. I think that in spite of all the love and good intentions in the world, we are so deeply harmed when we aren't allowed to simply give voice to our experience, and even more so when we aren't allowed to question "the way things are." I have no doubt that, as a child, I needed to learn how to modulate my reactions appropriately. What I learned instead was to suppress my emotions and accept whatever was happening to me without question or complaint.

Adam Zagajewski's "Try to Praise the Mutilated World" is a poem that I've tried to internalize. I should say that it's a poem that I aspire to in a lot of different ways. It doesn't shy away from anything. It's honest about the ugliness of the world, how hateful it is. It's honest about how hard it is to look at a world like that, especially with patience and compassion. But it does. And it assures us that there's something accomplished in that very struggle. So I guess if I were to give any sort of advice to other writes struggling with brutal questions, it would be to keep struggling. And maybe read Zagajewski.

Kimberly Povloski is a poet from Houston, Texas. They graduated from Eastern Washington University's MFA program in 2018.

The title of this collection, *hell of birds*, is lifted from the painting, *Hölle der Vögel*, by Max Beckmann.

OTHER DRIFTWOOD PRESS TITLES

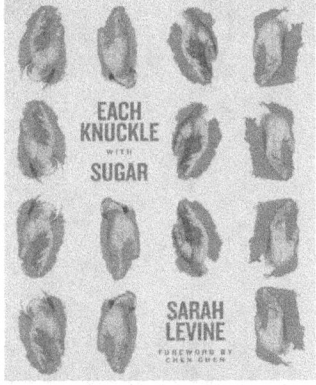

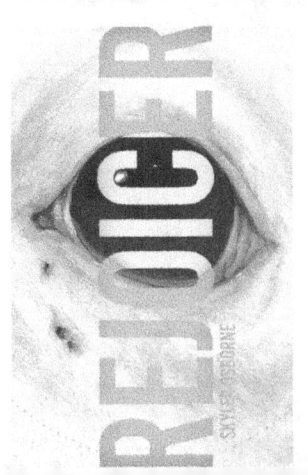

www.ingramcontent.com/pod-product-compliance
Lightning Source LLC
Chambersburg PA
CBHW052107110526
44591CB00013B/2387